Isle

Isle

TEXT Rena Rosenwasser

DRAWINGS Kate Delos

KELSEY ST. PRESS 1992

Acknowledgments:
Some of these poems have appeared in *Central Park*, *Motel*, and *Hanging Loose*
Book Design by Robert Rosenwasser

Rosenwasser, Rena, 1950-
Isle — Poetry— Rena Rosenwasser ; Drawings— Kate Delos.
P. CM
ISBN: 0-932716-28-8 : $12.95 —
ISBN: 0-932716-29-6 (50 limited signed with original drawing by the artist): $40
I. Delos, Kate, 1945 - . II. Title.
PS3568.08414318 1992
811' .54--dc20   91-43512
                                              CIP

Dedication:
I am grateful to Patricia Dienstfrey, Barbara Guest, Denise Lawson Fox, Elizabeth Robinson and Renate Stendhal for their insights and comments.

Part I

Isle

On this island
                              the loose dirt path. I skirt it
and we wind around, myself and this impulse for ruins. Rock
roses low to the ground. The high pitch of crickets.
Where is the small settlement found?   My arms flail at my sides.
Trailing. Loosely construed, they too are a mystery. Cover or uncover
signal.

Here the path parts, right or left. No markers to indicate where
exactly the English dug. A small settlement somewhere. Second
millenium. B.C. Go right then.

                                        Right now I trust. Lustral
basin, kitchen, simple votive terracotta. A large clay figurine,
her arms raised.   And the stirrup pot, spout with eyes. The Museum
called it Camaran.   I was led to believe

Preparation of purple dye.   From the shell,
Murex trunculus

*****

                                        Each island
its own clean page.   This morning I step onto the bus marked Red
beach, Akrotiri.

See how bleached white and empty the island is. How many pages
do I have and here I draw another line, underline myself on

another isle. See how little there is on this island. Small unruly grapes.

My eyes skim pottery shards, feel the jagged cracked places.
When they say Pre-Greek what is it. This un-ciphered,
meaning to break an alphabet or break

letter(s).

                    At the site I am reminded of something not fixed, not set
into place, half opened,

cut into the hillside. A metal awning protects excavated
places from

further slides.   I stepped in and lost the familiar
Mediterranean

light

When I awoke all the white buildings molded
out of the cliffs shimmered. When I walked over to

two small glass doors that exited out onto a deck my eyes fell
over skim

milk white Cycladic roofs and
porches and slim ultramarine window frames   then
down

down into rivulets of cobalt water. The sky above pale egg shell
blue. Soft air under my fingertips leaned over the balcony and then
below another balcony and then another.
All similarly placed

Inside the site
damp clay. The color of earthenware prevails; it is everywhere,
the ground, the walls, the broken pots. Russet, almost brown.
Madder. Thin rails say go here, don't go there. The ruins of ancient
residences barred. My eyes find the way through door jambs, window
frames. Cracked walls and floors an almost penetrable red. The houses
stacked one upon another, fallen in places.   Here so near shore

An ancient village . . . what was it they had dug soft
pumice

        >>>>
<< <

>>>

     100 meters down through soft pumice and then they came
to walls, ceilings, stone floor. Why dig here?   Was it the unusual
intrigue?   More than the usual shards of cracked pots.
                              Later I find they found
fragments of shattered fresco. Ancient colors strewn on stone floor
when the volcano buried the town.

      >>
<<<<
        >>>

         I follow a narrow path.
This, probably a thoroughfare for the ancient town and this larger area,
a public square. Enormous pots, painted with swirling lines, strewn
off to the side.
Some upright. Others tilt. A communal share of olive oil.
Wine. But the people had
disappeared. No bones were ever found.   Fragments of painting
had fallen instead. The work of meticulously piecing together
frescoes over entire walls.

Shattered and now reformed. Lines drawn and continued in the
present form the suppositions of what is lost.

Two adolescents wrestle. Their bodies narrow,
sparsely clad, long wavy black

                              hair; the lines of the drawing sinuous,
their sex in

de terminate.

I go all the way through

                      the site. Exit
at another point into the intense outer light.

Once more I walk around
                                    enter where I had begun
and now other groups with tour guides and voices appear inside
the damp redness.

There are German voices and French. They gather in
tightly closed groups. I slip in among them on the inside
listening.

Afternoon, another matter.   As if I could begin
anew. Another paragraph perhaps.
I do not want to stop myself now, although
I leave enough space. I drive past a long black beach. There is a trail,
a simple road. They say the Ptolemies settled on the top
where there is a look-out, a fortified Point. Agora
and temples. I go up the steep slope, though I take it slowly.
And thyme takes hold   It is the sweetest thyme, this mountain
thyme

and then there's Thira

In the evening
when the light falters and I have read all there is to read
about the day. I open the pages of my notebooks and the
gaps open like the empty space in between the scrawl
of written words. And the light changes the color of the page. Russets,
pale tinted tones.

The paper's ground looks more the color of clay and that
brittle.

****

Placements. Now I

                              fold the scattered clothes and books
into the steel grey luggage. Expand, contract as wings
of one more flight create distance. The lapses of take-offs and landings.
Maps with perimeters that fall

on another isle.

I had created distance, unknown terrain divorced from familiar
language between lovers and friends.
Only these

unutterances.

Another set
with its possible directions

                    This island larger than the
last. The hotel is on the Bay of Mirabello
and when I check in I am given a key, a mailbox.
The box is empty. Instead there is a vast bed, a desk,
a deck. All facing east. I decide to begin with a route to
the furthest ruin in that direction.
At dawn I wake, I find my map. I follow the line of the shore
and watch two sets of blues merge
Aegean and Sky

The hills themselves have a solid contour as I swerve round
curve after curve.   Changing

Once more driving

                              >>>>>>>

Signs indicate more of my Minoans. Mohklos . . .
Gournia, a settlement dating back to the third millenium.
Once there were narrow cobbled streets. Now weeds push
through broken stone.

I drive through the space called Kriti.
The country grows barer and the towns more austere. Olive
trees cling to the hills. I climb one more hill
and then screech down a precipice.
This must be Zagros.

                                                  It is the tip,
a beach. I walk bare
feet against broken white shells. Behind me is a path to
ruins and so I go

                    there, where there is a gate, an entrance fee
and here again the *Guide Bleu* has many pages to tell me where
and again I see an immense rectangular court.
Palace rooms splay off in all directions following
the contours of the land, rambling up the hillside on the one hand
and on the other leaning into the sea.

And when the sea tide comes in it fills the wells.

    The diagram on the page is complex. Am I here or where

the tablets were? I walk around what remains, room after
small room.   I have the sense of contours and
open
                              volumes. Space without

ceiling. If I stand

in the middle of the vast hall and face the sea
what I want should be behind me. I turn and find the place
that fits. It is a snug fit but I see when I enter where Platon found
the tablets. Some were crushed, others in perfect shape.
And this place, another space where he dug
   >>>>

      <<<
a libation cup   forms of double axes on the surface. I trace

                    retrace, weave back and this must be
the well where

the well, why the sea water would wash over
and fill the well where they found submerged another cup. Inside
were perfectly preserved olives. Three thousand year old
olives and when the excavators looked at what they had unveiled
the substance disappeared. The fruit vanished and the skin
shrivelled before their eyes.

                              The story line appears and

   disappears.

         Linear A. Somewhere a lost
language. What's left etched on these tablets. When the
walls fell words broke. Patterns move and can be constructed,
reconstructed. But where do lines lead that are seen but
not deciphered. My own words stumble; they too lose direction

sign >>>s.

                        More and more of my nights are
carved out of drawings on pithoi. Double

axes lean back to back. Butterfly wings on either side of a woman
drawn in the shape of a bee. Bulls' horns, two, above her head.
If I turn the horns on their sides and place them
back to back,

stare and squint, will something come back to me?

A fluid field. More double axes. Cretan idyll. Turn   and
turn over

                        One form and then another. A miniature
piece. Two birds crown pillars which form a swing. A woman
swings. Her skirt painted with chevrons; they
>>>>>>
<<<<

the white clay surface.   Pillars and base form horns
atop a flat cranial surface.   What was that game
they used to play?
Swing, swing over the horns.

                                If I swing will forms
regroup?

            I open another book to prevent myself from

        >>
<<<<<
between my hands. I lift the stiff outer cover and turn
the light pages. Press down.

*****

       Here on Kriti time is so old. It isn't like any I've been
taught to count. The thermometer stays the same but time
skids off

              Skid a little. At the summit road work, loose
rocks. Another tractor, submission to machinery. Parched throat

over the precipice. The window reveals.

Karphi, Rousikiana. I am looking for a cave at Psichro. Slip
down cliffs and then fertile fields where fruit trees grow in rows.
Apricots or are these pistachios? I look for markers.
Green signs

Late. More mid middle . . . What time was that? Kronos' Rhea's
Z's time. Z whose full name I have chosen not to mention though
they say he was born inside this cave.

Legend has it . . .

What does legend have

Open mouths. A long slippery descent. How many meters down?
Soon I find my way, candle-lit, an exquisite wish to undress
my eyes. Now truly open the aperture wider and wider. There is so
little light as I descend. Why not dig my fingers in.
Let go just a little dis place   space

Don't slip

Be precise. Measure pleasure   Who was dipped inside this
puddle? How wet was it then when C a v e meant primary place.
Illuminate a stalactite. << See

her likeness>>   Look up and now I am further in Up there. Trees
around the rim, soft tangle of branches. My descent exposes
me more and

lower in the dark envelope

*****

Another day. This time I know I will go where all the tourists
go, but I decide to arrive early. It is Sunday
and the main highway deserted. I do not stop. No tavernas.
No stuffed grape leaves and tzatziki salad.
I am not at all like the lines that meander. Now I inhabit an American
space. Expedient. Not one wrong turn.
The sign says I'm there. The lot is empty and the gate
is shut tight. There is a strike, it says, come back tomorrow.

*****

                                        Far away
from anybody I knew and there were only letters. I could create
my own or stand and stare, moved to fill in the blank spaces
in between the rocks, the caves, the folds of paper

                                                    I felt an absence
in the empty envelopes. Although I had my own alphabet to send
away. Cast off and out they might take a hydroplane or an aeroplane.
How long would they take to land?

Familiar hands tear open seals. An alphabet of antique
tears

escape as my easily ciphered A's and B's roll off familiar tongues

When I sleep Minoan meanders move across the surface. The black
lines erupt without any tangible reason. There are no
broken pots in the dreams, no antique, unciphered tablets.
Nothing to actually grab hold of and when I walked inside the ruin
the wall was just a little bit taller than I was
and it was full of wavy lines.

And here the wall is also about my size and full of similar
strokes.   Her hair or his. So much alike. A kind of confusion
in   Long black curlicues.

These people of the sea drew everything in waves.
What happened to them?   Who were those
others in the low prowed boats with the long shields

Go inside. Get wet

                        Seas

                        Sea peoples

  Zagros, >>>>>
>>> Knossos. Palatial possibilities. Expand and contract in fluid fields.
Swollen lines. How many readings are there? Here I'm left with a need
to place words, w/ out a sound, on paper.

              When I wrote letters the days had the voice of intimacy;
they were so close I could hear them breathe
in my hands. Who are you out there that I want to hold you like
a sheet of paper and create letters that disassemble
as you open the envelope and
                  each day opens when I go to the desk in my
hotel room there is always a possibility that letters will come
to me from

out outside

                        <<<<<<

>>>>>

<<<<<<

More than the middle of the Minoans.   More than middle or
middle late I keep on following the trail. They lived on these shores
and made many pots, paintings. Were they artisans, traders of wool

                creators of labyrinthian structures that provoked
many tales

or is the labyrinth only a labyrinth if the tellers of the tale misconstrued
the space of this elaborate double-axed relationship

Will I tell you in these letters how
                      the horizon keeps drifting further away

No don't stop at the corner. Let's not end where the page runs
out of room. Even if the envelope is empty the air inside
damp, reverberates

       How many excavated places are there opened un-
opened
    >>>>

                They found libation cups on
Peak sanctuaries. One day when I walked inadvertently higher
up . . . it was green, here near Lithakia, and the rock was limestone
and I kept going on and on looking for a cave and I lost sight of
grapes and I lost sight of goats and lost

Ends
like the end of the frescoes that wound round losing sight of the
walls' ends

how will we live in this other spatial relationship when I lose
track and

                        for a moment the letters and the isles and the day
empties of English and my eyes lean

South, here even oranges grow and Egypt is not far
off

                            More than leaving off the openings   w/ out
salutations on the paper, absence

close to the skin.

Note

The opening quote from Art ex Absentia, *Bojana Pejic,* Art Forum, *April 1990. Translated from the Serbo-Croatian by Ivan Vejvoda.*

Part II

Grass

If she were able to lie flat like grass in wind   Shutter
gently & at random

                              That's how   carried forward
in light shade her desire falls   where skin
on her belly has traces of an exterior hand

More wind opens the outline of her body

pattern governed by chaos   A theory charted
like fluids

Coincidence at the end of the curves

exaggerate   as she herself   Blood   Water
Hair
on her skin   More extreme in taller tufted zones
                        Go over Panicles

the body slopes   deciduous   her lips call Deschampsia

Imperata

Rhizomatous   Sound divides memory
                        underground runners

Earth's Liquid Body

Richly flavored fluids   fino or superfino
perfect elemental fragrant   as I speak rice
in the spoon   In its primary stage un/

broken

broth

brew   battle with fluid decision
Shall it be a double one of bones and trimmings?

Fallen on the counter   dispel
wide-bellied

In the pot pearly descents

Don't let it go so low   slowly stir
How many minutes was it loose   a disposition
savory attitude
I like this going round without a drop in temperature

Small incidental   white kernel in the center
Capacity to

Stir   be s t i r r e d

When the final stage arrives what will it be?
Squid ink or octopus.   A composition —
in the asparagus bog
needled with bitter chicory, wild
thyme

my desire — leafy edge wedged in glutinous grain

Solid additions must be kept warm

before they blend
as mood blends e v e n i n g   An orange kernel
of sun

Garden Views

I. PARADEISOS
   (Greek, stocked with everything good and valuable, from old Persian, pairidaeza, enclosure or park)

   I pencilled in the garden
   cross///hatch —

         lavender   crayoned purples
            you held the spade

we blew torn remnants

   when we sat down on the chamomile bench air crushed
smell of removal

could we collage (in an extreme moment)
origins

      trees bearing fruit
                              persimmon, pomegranate
                        (original pear)

      with your expedient moves   your reasoned approach
            now lean over
our creation —

                        Rectangles, an enclosure or park,
furthermore I extended two lines to the top of the page

& then a loose scrawl.   Figuration
Rows   Shimmer of perfect
poplars

Pulled.

                    Leaves.   w/ out

        leave-taking

II. MEDIEVAL

hortyards of pears
pared down players   rush of garbed black over cold stone the body
with no time to wander
          discretionary, lit
by the niche in the cell

light white reason

     Core of the pear pared of its skin, juice of the fruit   NO
to the silly sweet feel   not cotton black but stiff woolen
safe without women

we had taken these medieval moments to mean a collection of
nays   ought nots   conjugate the body (bit by thorns)
discretionary as our selves, cellular
illumined

not a word misspent   order of the day   matins. lauds. sext coming
together only with Latin links

          (no to luggage — nay to the body's instinctual
largesse)

               strip away the necessity for fruit, tear eyes from fields
of Seckle, Poire d'Anjou

don't let ripples in   separate self & skin
Kneel

                                        pulchrum congruentia
a numerical balance beam pushed up to the highest measure
the mind rises   plays a game of perfect spheres

left below
        archaic
                                offed to the sides   p(e)
a i r s

III. BAROQUE GARDENS

the imagination scrawls bitter
greens
                            How will we compose ourselves

You say *Basilico*   I say, *Necessary hint*
Plant the tongue & run

                along Italy's
            purple veins

chatter of crinolines   we pitched the loose ball
over a flourish of geometry

    to break ground
            parterre

                            (hedged
propositions)   navigate circles and squares

through the center   the path pulls
further   u p

extravagant frenzy of the outer reaches

    slim portico
once more
        water whispers *Sibillare*

Lighter Metallic Elements
(Death Valley, 1990)

Not this warm if we were ever this warm.

Badwater the hottest place possible. Compounded
with infrequent and violent storms. I arrive

Mica and flexible

Would our hands hold ourselves
if our bodies inside our hands were ever this
Fill.

         * * *

Where the earth washes. Silt.

Shining salts. Easily separated particles from a certain point
of view. Crusty

buildup. Desire to evaporate.
Lift.

I have taken hikes. There is a color for them
When your shirt was this hiked up above your hands
Swept over. Alluvial

fan

Their lacquered faces red and slippery
[for PMC]

I.
Screens slide open. You open your intimate
interior. A single flower appears.

Is this perennial movement of lips? I form wind red
rustles. Soft scratch of stalks surrounds a furniture of scarcity.

Here where all usual places are absence.

II.
I like the drift of this alternative narrative marked by missing.

The body within arrangement . . . is it the oriental matter
of another climate or have we moved to
a traditional $\ln(n)$.

Inside room's small frame.   Our borders grow fuzzy.

How many layers lacquer the bowl smooth as the tea ceremony.

III.
When I close my eyes
the monk bends over the exterior garden. He listens to pebbles
rake as his thoughts wander through pine.

Gravity lighter than air.

Fermented dampness. If I robe the afternoon will taste moss green

reveal more gradations of grey between needles

Unlikely

Speech to Aspen

Branches whisper *weather*   Mercury falls somewhere snow
In your white wrap with a hint of ash black knots
escape   Air from the center leaves a trail   Revery is easy

What of this perpetual exaggerated impulse to extend
over the snow   *Not now* she whispers to herself
not now   She remembers the story of a man who drew peculiar
mechanical wings   Images have always followed this story
His drawings poised on the edge of her every precipice

When she thinks of these pictures they link, a long in-
escapable chain, like logic   She wants to dispel
memory   Up here only bare trees w/out the necessity of
lucid invention

Aspens seed and reseed   She talks to layers of bark
twist turn   The lift lifts further up   Is this the coating
that covers the world   torso of the tree with mysterious
wrappers   (bandaged) listen to the wrappers

sshhhhh   sshuhhh   hisss
shisss

with each inch ground falls away air begins to sway
desire to be in white casement   Imagine blistered linens
like love   Mummies push up   ancient
ease or *trees*

ISLE is a limited edition of
one thousand copies;
fifty numbered, signed by the artists with an original
hand-colored print on Wyndstone Facade paper.
Printed at West Coast Print Center on Mohawk Superfine
paper with drawings on Johannot,
Crescent endpaper and Paloma Matte coverstock.
Gill Sans typeface. Typesetting by Access Typography.
Design by Robert Rosenwasser.

Kelsey St. Press, 1992.